THE FULFILLMENT OF ALL DESIRE
STUDY GUIDE

Ralph Martin
with *Emily Stimpson*

EMMAUS
ROAD
PUBLISHING

Steubenville, Ohio

ο

Emmaus Road Publishing
1468 Parkview Circle
Steubenville, OH 43952

© 2010 by Ralph Martin
All rights reserved. Published 2010
Printed in the United States of America
7th Printing 2018

Library of Congress Control Number: 2010928688
ISBN: 978-1-931018-60-9

Unless otherwise indicated, Scripture quotations are taken
from the Revised Standard Version, Catholic Edition (RSVCE) © 1965, 1966
by the Division of Christian Education of the National Council of the Churches
of Christ in the United States of America. Used by permission.

Scripture texts cited in the text as "NAB" are taken from the
New American Bible with Revised New Testament and Revised Psalms © 1991, 1986, 1970
Confraternity of Christian Doctrine, Washington, D.C. and are used by permission
of the copyright owner. All rights reserved. No part of the *New American Bible*
may be reproduced in any form without permission
in writing from the copyright owner.

Excerpts from the English translation of the
Catechism of the Catholic Church for the United States of America © 1994,
United States Catholic Conference, Inc. —Libreria Editrice Vaticana.
English translation of the *Catechism of the Catholic Church:
Modifications from the Editio Typica* © 1997, United States Catholic Conference, Inc.
—Libreria Editrice Vaticana. Cited in the text as "CCC."

Cover design and layout by
Theresa Westling

Cover artwork:
Thomas Cole, *The Pilgrim of the Cross at the End of His Journey*
Smithsonian American Art Museum / Art Resources NY

CONTENTS

INTRODUCTION

In this world, every person is on a journey. That journey either leads us to God—to heaven, holiness, and eternal happiness—or it leads us away from God, to the hell that is separation from Him.

Each step we take on this journey has eternal weight, eternal consequences, which is why, through the centuries, those who've traversed the path to holiness successfully have offered the rest of us wisdom and counsel about how to do the same. Through their homilies, letters, theological treatises, and spiritual autobiographies, these saints communicated their own experience of living in relationship with God. They also charted the course from sin to glory, mapping out the steps we each must take to reach our desired end.

That course is the focus of *The Fulfillment of All Desire*. As the subtitle states, the book is "A Guidebook for the Journey to God Based on the Wisdom of the Saints"—meaning that the book is, in effect, a roadmap to the roadmap of the saints. It collects and connects the wisdom of seven of the Church's greatest teachers, detailing their thoughts on renouncing sin, growing in faith and virtue, and embracing the graces God gives for our salvation.

That wisdom, however, is vast and mysterious. Probing its depths is the work of a lifetime, and understanding it requires careful reading, studied reflection, and above all, prayer. That is where this study guide comes in. It is as much a roadmap to *The Fulfillment of All Desire* as *The Fulfillment of All Desire* is a roadmap to the wisdom of the saints.

—⁓—

HOW TO USE THIS BOOK

Chapter by chapter, this study guide walks you through the main points of each stage of the spiritual journey. It also helps you apply what you've read to your own walk. For each chapter in the book, there is a chapter in the study guide that offers a quick summary of the chapter's content, as well as a series of objective questions that, when answered, will help you master the basic points presented.

Each chapter in the study guide also includes several questions for reflection or discussion. There are no right answers to those questions. They're simply intended to help you think more deeply about how you can benefit from the saints' insight and counsel. Also included in each chapter is further information about the saints or Church teachings that relate to the subject matter covered, as well as an index of key terms. At the back of the study guide, you'll find a glossary containing concise definitions of all those important words and phrases.

This study guide can be used as part of a small group or parish study, in a college or high school classroom, or as an aid to your own reading. Regardless of where you use it, however, the key to using it well is to begin your reading and reflecting with prayer. Also, take your time. Read not just for knowledge, but also for understanding. Don't rush through the questions (notice that there is no answer key). And as you both read and reflect, ask God to help you apply the saints' counsel to the challenges you face right now, in your journey today.

I offer that advice not because the book is difficult to understand: it's not. But living the message it contains can be difficult. Sin, selfishness, and self-deception don't immediately disappear when we start our journey to God. But the good news—the good news that the saints repeat in every chapter of *The Fulfillment of All Desire*—is that ultimately, it's not up to us to become saints. We don't make ourselves holy. God makes us holy. It is His work, not ours. All we have to do is ask for His help, be open to His help, and cooperate with Him as that help is given.

I pray that both this study guide and the book itself help you to do just that and in some small way lead you closer to that which you're seeking—the fulfillment of all desire.

Chapter One

CALLED TO HOLINESS

Summary

During His time on earth, Christ called His followers to "be perfect, as your heavenly Father is perfect" (Mt. 5:48). That call to perfection is, essentially, a call to holiness, a call to sainthood.

For two thousand years, the Church has continued calling God's sons and daughters to sainthood. And in recent decades, that call has come with even greater urgency. From the Second Vatican Council's focus on "the universal call to holiness" to Pope John Paul II's landmark apostolic letter *Novo Millenio Ineunte*, the Church has proclaimed with increasing frequency and clarity the need for all Christians—lay as well as religious— to "be perfect, as your heavenly Father is perfect."

The urgency of that proclamation stems, in part, from the world's need for saints. In a culture that has strayed farther and farther from its Christian roots, the wholehearted witness of believers is essential. More important than the world's need, however, is our own need. We need to become saints. It's why God made us.

Before time began, God destined us for union with Him. We exist so that we might live in love forever with Him. His grace makes that possible. All we have to do is dispose ourselves to receive that grace. We have to choose to receive it. We have to choose to see all the obstacles and difficulties we encounter in life as opportunities for grace, opportunities for growth. And we have to turn to Jesus again and again, contemplating His face and asking for His help.

Ultimately, there are only two possible ends to the story of our life: eternal joy in heaven with God or eternal suffering apart from God in Hell. That is why we can't put off our pursuit of holiness. The pursuit must begin now.

Questions for Comprehension

1. What was one of the main rediscoveries to which the Holy Spirit led the Church through the Second Vatican Council?

2. What does it really mean to ask someone, "Do you wish to receive baptism?"

3. What does "holiness" mean? Define it.

4. What did John Paul II say parishes must become in the twenty-first century? What did he mean by that?

5. According to John Paul II, what are three reasons why it is important for Christians to respond to the universal call to holiness?

6. Why is a recovery of the Church's mystical traditions a necessary part of answering the call to holiness?

7. What four principles must we keep in mind in order to have a proper understanding of the spiritual journey?

8. What really holds us back from answering the call to holiness?

9. What is the ultimate source of all our unhappiness?

10. What is the purpose of our creation? How are we made ready for that purpose?

Questions for Reflection

1. Do you struggle to believe that it's possible for you to "be perfect, as your heavenly Father is perfect"? Why or why not?

2. Part of our journey to God involves being healed of the wounds of sin—both original sin and the sins we've personally committed. What wounds or bad habits do you need to ask God to heal so that you can grow closer to Him?

3. Do you ever find yourself putting off the pursuit of holiness for a "better" time? How do you rationalize that delay to yourself? In other words, what are some of the excuses you make?

4. What circumstances in your life today feel like obstacles to the pursuit of holiness? How can those obstacles actually become opportunities for growing closer to God?

5. What are some ways you can begin contemplating the face of Christ in the midst of your ordinary, day-to-day life?

More About—The Jubilee Year

Every twenty-five years the Catholic Church commemorates the redeeming death of Christ and the fruits of His Resurrection by proclaiming a Year of Jubilee. A great religious event, the year is intended to be a year of forgiveness, reconciliation, and conversion for all people.

The tradition of the Jubilee goes back to the time of Moses. In Leviticus 25:10–14, God instructed the Israelites to set aside one year out of every fifty in which debts would be forgiven, slaves freed, land returned to its original owners, and families restored to one another.

Christians resumed the practice of the Jubilee Year in 1300. In the wake of wars and diseases that had ravaged Europe, a large group of pilgrims journeyed to Rome seeking the Pope's blessing and intending to pray for themselves and the world. The pope, Boniface VIII, rewarded their faith by declaring 1300 "A Holy Year" and a year "of the forgiveness of all sins."

In the centuries since, the tradition continued, with Jubilees occurring at first every fifty years, then eventually, every twenty-five. The Jubilees that now occur every twenty-five years are referred to as "ordinary" Jubilee Years. Extraordinary Jubilee Years are those called for some outstanding reason, such as the Jubilee Year that Pope Pius XI proclaimed in 1933 to mark the 1900th anniversary of man's redemption.

The year 2000 marked the first Jubilee Year to occur at the turn of the millennium. It also marked the 2,000[th] anniversary of the birth of Christ. For those reasons, Pope John Paul II believed the Holy Spirit would bless the Church with a special outpouring of graces and that those graces would equip the Church for the challenges of the new millennium. Accordingly, countless special celebrations were planned in Rome and around the world that year, while a special indulgence was offered to all Catholics who made a holy pilgrimage during the year. By the end of 2000 an estimated thirty-two million people had journeyed to Rome.

Key Terms ————————————————————————————

Beatific Vision
Original Sin

Chapter Two

AN OVERVIEW OF THE JOURNEY

Summary

Growing in holiness is truly a journey. It's a journey from self to God, from sin to sanctity, from worshipping the things of the world to worshipping the things of heaven. It's also a journey that takes time. We don't spiritually progress from love of self to love of God overnight. As with any journey, there are different phases, or stages, through which we pass.

Through the centuries, different spiritual writers have attempted to classify these stages. Although they have labeled and grouped the stages of the spiritual life somewhat differently, in essence their classifications are the same. Generically, these stages are described as the *purgative*, *illuminative*, and *unitive* ways.

Questions for Comprehension

1. What happens to a soul during the purgative stage? List five phases that characterize this stage.

2. What happens to a soul during the illuminative stage? List seven characteristics of this stage.

3. What experiences typically accompany the illuminative stage?

4. What typically happens to a soul in the unitive way? List five characteristics of this stage.

5. How is suffering different in the unitive stage?

6. What terminology does St. Teresa of Avila use to classify the different spiritual stages?

7. What three names does St. John of the Cross assign to souls in the three different stages?

8. What three attitudes does St. Catherine of Sienna attribute to souls in the different stages of the spiritual life?

9. How does St. Bernard of Clairvaux characterize the feelings experienced by souls as they progress in their journey to God?

10. According to St. Francis de Sales, what purpose do the emotions experienced by souls in the purgative and illuminative stages still play once a soul has entered the unitive stage?

Questions for Reflection

1. Did you experience an initial conversion or an awakening of faith? How did your first years as a believer reflect the characteristics of the purgative stage?

2. After your initial conversion what sins did you have to break away from? What habits of virtue and piety did you have to work to acquire? What habits of virtue and piety are you still struggling to acquire?

3. With the passing of time, how has your faith grown and changed? What spiritual challenges do you face now that you didn't face in the beginning of your journey to God?

More About—Doctors of the Church

When it comes to honors bestowed by the Catholic Church, there are few more distinguished or harder to come by than that of being declared a Doctor of the Church. In the entire history of Christianity, only thirty-three men and women have earned that title. But what does this designation mean?

The title itself dates back to the early fifth century, when Rufus of Aquileia used the term to describe a great teacher of the faith. The title remained a fluid and informal one until the thirteenth century when the Church formalized the process for declaring a person a "Doctor of the Church." From that point on, in order to be honored with the title, "Doctor," a person must have demonstrated exemplary holiness; deepened the whole Church's understanding of the Catholic faith; and been officially declared a Doctor via papal proclamation.

Also in the thirteenth century, the Church clarified who was and who was not a Doctor of the Church. The initial list included St. Gregory the Great, St. Jerome, St. Ambrose, and St. Augustine. Not long after, four eminent teachers from the East were added to the list: St. John Chrysostom, St. Basil of Caesarea, St. Gregory of Nazianzus, and St. Athanasius.

Over the past eight hundred years, twenty-five men and women have been added to their company. The list now includes bishops, priests, and deacons, as well as two popes, several founders or reformers of religious orders, and a handful of mystics. Ten Doctors were added to the list in the twentieth century alone, including, for the first time, three women: St. Catherine of Siena, St. Theresa of Avila, and St. Thérèse of Lisieux.

Key Terms

Illuminative Way
Purgative Way
Unitive Way

Chapter Three

AWAKENINGS AND CONVERSION

Summary

Every journey of faith has a beginning, and the lessons learned at that beginning can help direct the journey to its proper end. The lives of both St. Teresa of Avila and St. Augustine bear witness to that.

St. Teresa's journey began with an awakening, a moment in time where her eyes were opened to the greatness of God's grace and the tragedy of her own lack of generosity. For forty years, she lived the life of a lukewarm Catholic. In those first forty years, she did experience moments of awareness and inspiration—moments where God gave her a profound sense of His presence and moments where she resolved to give her life to Him. Those moments were powerful enough to inspire her to join the Carmelites at the age of twenty. They were not, however, enough to guard her against the lukewarmness she encountered even behind the convent's walls.

Reflecting on her early life, Teresa blamed her lack of progress in the spiritual life on four things: she didn't understand the cumulative danger of small sins; she didn't avoid situations that could lead her to sin; she wasn't grateful enough for the moments of grace and inspiration God gave her; and she relied too much on herself and not enough on God. Only when she recognized those four failings as the obstacles they were, could she move forward on the path to holiness.

Unlike Teresa, St. Augustine's journey towards God began not with an awakening, but rather with a conversion—a radical rejection of his past beliefs and actions and the acceptance of a new way of life.

Although Augustine's mother, Monica, was a Christian, his father was not, and it was his father's ways not his mother's that Augustine initially followed. As a young man, Augustine developed an abiding interest in philosophy, and pursued a career as a teacher and scholar. He cared about truth and, at least in theory, he wanted to know and live by the truth. But that desire was not as strong as his desire for women. Augustine rebelled against the idea of chastity and refused to consider it.

As the years passed, however, Augustine moved closer and closer to the Christian faith. God used all the circumstances of Augustine's life—his interest in literature and philosophy, the disappointments of the world, and the faith of his mother—to bring him to the point of conversion. But even when he was convinced of the truth of Christianity, Augustine still struggled to embrace it. The habits of sin were etched deep in Augustine's soul. Those habits had become such a part of his life that he didn't know how to live without them. But, thanks in large part to the witness and testimony of others and, in even larger part to God's grace, Augustine finally surrendered those sins to God and embraced the faith he had long believed true.

In that surrender, Augustine bore witness to the same truth that St. Teresa experienced in her awakening: grace is the foundation of our relationship with God. We can never achieve holiness on our own, nor can we reject sin by our own efforts. Grace begins it all.

Questions for Comprehension

1. What are the dangers of a "lukewarm" faith?

2. What is the difference between deliberately chosen venial sin and inadvertent venial sin? How can venial sins become a serious obstacle to holiness?

3. Define the term "near occasion of sin." How do these "occasions" lead us away from God?

4. How can too much self-reliance discourage us from pursuing holiness?

5. How does St. Francis de Sales define the devout life? How can appreciating the graces God gives us help us to lead that sort of life?

6. In what ways can an incorrect understanding of God become an obstacle to faith?

7. Describe the importance of personal witness and testimony to Augustine's conversion. Who were some of the witnesses who helped him on his journey? What made their testimony so powerful?

8. What is the primary obstacle that prevented Augustine from embracing the Christian faith?

9. According to St. Thérèse of Lisieux, whom does God forgive more: those who have committed serious sins or those who have never committed serious sins? Explain.

10. What do both John Paul II and St. Teresa say is a constant temptation for people as they progress in the faith? How does that temptation impede true holiness? How should we see all occasions for serving God and doing good?

Questions for Reflection

1. Describe the beginnings of your own faith journey. Have you always had a strong faith or did you embrace a relationship with Christ through an awakening or conversion? What are some of the lessons you learned at the beginning of your journey that have helped you along the way?

2. Reflect upon the four obstacles that impeded St. Teresa's growth in holiness. Have you encountered those same obstacles? Which ones? Which of those obstacles do you still struggle with? Explain.

3. Who are some of the witnesses that have helped you move closer to God? What did they say or do that helped you?

4. St. Augustine delayed embracing the Christian faith because he couldn't bring himself to renounce serious and habitual sins. Is there any sin in your life right now that is holding you back from fully and freely living the faith? If so, how have

you excused or justified your behavior? How are those excuses harming you?

5. When it comes to practicing the virtues and pursuing sanctity, do you ever find yourself relying more on yourself than on God? If so, why do you think that is? What needs to happen to change that?

In Brief—St. Augustine

Born—November 13, AD 354 in Thagaste, a town now part of Eastern Algeria in North Africa.

Family—Son of St. Monica (a devout Christian who spent decades praying for the conversion of her son and husband) and Patricius (a pagan, opposed to his wife's faith, but who was eventually baptized on his deathbed in AD 372); Father of Adeodatus, his son by his longtime mistress. Adeodatus came into the Church with his father in AD 387, then died two years later, at the age of seventeen.

Converted—in AD 387, after several years of wrestling with the claims of the Christian faith. He was baptized by St. Ambrose in Milan, Italy.

Worked—as a teacher of grammar in Thagaste (AD 372–373), a professor of rhetoric in Carthage, North Africa (AD 373–

384), and professor of rhetoric for the Imperial Court in Milan (AD 384–387).

Served—for four years as a priest in the North African coastal diocese of Hippo-Regius, then as bishop of Hippo until his death.

Combated—just about every major Christian heresy of the early Church, including Pelagianism, Arianism, Donatism, and Manicheanism.

Wrote—*Confessions, On Christian Doctrine, City of God*, and the *Enchiridion*, as well as many other books and thousands of sermons, over three hundred of which remain in existence.

Died—August 28, AD 430.

Feast Day—August 28.

Key Terms

Grace

THE BIBLICAL WORLDVIEW OF THE SAINTS

Summary

Understanding the spiritual wisdom of the saints requires that we understand their vision of reality—of heaven and hell, and all they contain. That vision is the foundation from which they teach. And it is a vision fundamentally shaped by Sacred Scripture.

For saints such as Catherine of Siena, Bernard of Clairvaux, and John of the Cross, the vision begins with the end—the end of each individual man. Ultimately, two possible ends await us— heaven or hell. Heaven is the fulfillment of all desire, the place where we look upon the face of God and live in perfect friendship with all those we loved in life who died in friendship with Christ. Hell is a place of eternal regret, where we look upon the face of the devil and are tormented by past sins.

Drawing from Sacred Scripture, those saints teach that there is but one way to heaven: Jesus Christ. Through a relationship with Him and by God's mercy, we can traverse the difficult and narrow path to heaven.

Although love should define our relationship with God, that love should originate in the "fear of the Lord"—in a proper respect for God's goodness and a proper understanding of our own sinfulness. That fear is the beginning of both wisdom and love, and acts as a check on foolish or wrong behavior throughout our earthly life.

Scripture also shaped St. Catherine and St. John's understanding of human choice and free will. Both recognized that heaven and hell are choices, and that the souls dwelling in both are dwelling there because of their own freely made decisions. Those who chose good throughout their life, chose heaven. Those who chose evil, chose hell. And God accepted those choices.

Because none of us know the day or the hour when death will come and the time for choosing will end, we must not delude ourselves about the reality of heaven and hell or the gravity of our own sin. We must love now, reject sin now, and trust in God's mercy now. Only by taking that path—the one described by Christ as "narrow" and found by "few" (Mt. 7:13–14)—can we avoid drifting with the culture along the path to Hell. And only by keeping the two possible ends of our life in mind, can we continually choose the end that will lead us to joy.

Questions for Comprehension

1. Describe the image that God gave St. Catherine of Siena to explain the structure of reality. What was the image and what did it mean?

2. What, according to St. Catherine's *Dialogues*, are the four principle torments of hell?

3. Why is the sight of the devil so terrible for the damned?

4. Define "fear of the Lord."

5. How does one acquire true wisdom?

6. What are some of the blessings and privileges given to souls in heaven?

7. What, according to St. Bernard, leads to growing confidence in God's love?

8. According to St. John of the Cross, what conclusions must a soul reach before seriously pursuing holiness and heaven?

9. What is the purpose of focusing on biblical passages about salvation, damnation, and the gravity of sin?

10. What is the "big picture" St. Teresa of Avila presumes people must understand in order to progress in the spiritual life? What will keeping that "big picture" in mind do for people?

Questions for Reflection

1. Reflect upon your own relationship with God. Do you fear Him in any way? Describe that fear. Is that fear the healthy fear of the Lord described in this chapter or is it another kind of fear?

2. Has there been a time where a healthy fear of the Lord has prevented you from making an unwise choice? If so, describe what happened. Next, describe an unwise choice that a healthier fear of the Lord could have prevented you from making. In what specific ways can a fear of the Lord help you lead a more virtuous life?

3. What choices are you making now that could lead you to choose hell? What choices are you making that could lead you to choose heaven? Based upon the sum total of choices you've

made in your life thus far, where do you think you would choose to go if you died today—heaven or hell?

4. Reread Matthew 7:13–14. How do Jesus' words conflict with cultural attitudes about heaven and hell? With whom do you find yourself agreeing more on this point—Jesus or the culture? How do your actions reflect your beliefs?

5. In what ways does the culture in which you live pull you away from the "narrow" road that leads to heaven? What aspects of the culture do you still need to reject in order to proceed down the road of the "few"?

In Brief—St. Catherine of Siena

Born—In 1347 in Siena, Italy.

Family—The twenty-fourth of twenty-five children and the daughter of a prosperous wool merchant, Catherine never married nor did she enter religious life. She did, however, wear the habit of a Dominican tertiary (a lay Dominican living in the world).

Lived—from ages eighteen to twenty-one in complete solitude in her father's house, leaving her room to do chores only after other family members had gone to bed. After entering into a spiritual marriage with Jesus, she renounced her solitude and began an active apostolate in the world.

Fasted—for most of her adult life, surviving primarily on the Eucharist.

Served—as an emissary of the Vatican to the cities of Pisa and Luca when war broke out between the Holy See and Florence in the mid 1370s.

Protested—the semi-permanent relocation of the pope to Avignon, France. Catherine wrote several letters to Gregory XI, before finally traveling to Avignon to make her case. Eventually, the pope conceded and returned to Rome.

Wrote—*The Dialogue*, an account of her conversations with God. Most of these conversations were dictated by Catherine to various secretaries.

Died—on April 29, 1380, while living in Rome. She had moved there several years earlier, at Pope Urban VI's request, to minister to him and his cardinals.

Feast Day—April 30.

Key Terms

Fear of the Lord

Chapter Five

THE TRANSFORMATION
OF THOUGHT, DESIRE, AND ACTION

Summary

The life of St. Thérèse of Lisieux exemplifies the inner transformation the pursuit of holiness brings about. As the young French Doctor of the Church grew closer to Christ, she took on the mind of Christ, learning to see the world and all it contained with His eyes and His love.

For Thérèse, that transformation began early. Blessed with devout and loving Catholic parents, Thérèse grew up in a home where the faith was at the center of daily life. Her parents and her older sisters not only instructed her in the faith, but also modeled the faith for her. They showed her what it meant to love and serve, trust and sacrifice. They also modeled the Father's love for her, surrounding her with their own love and helping her to understand how precious she was to both them and God.

From that cradle of perfect catechesis, St. Thérèse grew to desire the things of heaven more than the things of earth. Her earthly loves were purified and her greatest concerns became those of the Lord's. Pleasing Him, serving Him, and bringing souls to Him were her only desires. All those who journey close to God experience a similar transformation. As we grow in holiness, our desires, fears, and even our experience of joy changes.

The transformation of joy is particularly important. In a fallen world, we often rejoice in that which is not good, or we find our greatest joy in temporal goods. This disordered joy, which places too much value on the things of the world, puts us in spiritual danger and can ultimately lead us away from God. When joy is rightly ordered, however, and we learn to find our true joy in Christ, we also learn to find the right kind of joy in all the lesser goods of creation.

That is the kind of joy St. Thérèse experienced in life. It's also the kind of joy she has helped others to find.

Questions for Comprehension

1. What, according to St. Thérèse, is the greatest good that any person can wish for another?

2. In what ways did nature and the created world point St. Thérèse towards heaven?

3. List at least three ways that Thérèse's family helped bring her closer to God.

4. What was the role of the liturgy and the sacraments in Thérèse's spiritual transformation?

5. List two spiritual struggles of St. Thérèse as outlined in this chapter. For each, describe how she overcame that struggle.

6. According to St. John of the Cross, how does growing in holiness transform the emotion of fear?

7. List the six classes of goods in which St. John says we should rejoice. Briefly describe each class.

8. What are the four degrees of harm that can arise from taking inordinate joy in temporal goods?

9. What are the four "traits" or sins that correspondingly arise from each of those degrees of harm?

10. Describe what happens to those who deny themselves inordinate joy in temporal things. How is that possible?

Questions for Reflection

1. The Church often describes the family as a "school of faith." That was certainly true for St. Thérèse. Reflect on your own upbringing. In what ways did it help prepare you for your journey to God? In what ways, did it fall short of giving you the preparation you needed?

2. Name at least two ordinary created things or people that have helped you see God. Describe how they accomplished that.

3. Do you ever struggle with taking inordinate joy in temporal goods? What temporal goods? Why do you think this is a struggle for you?

4. Reflect upon the four traits that correspond to the four degrees of harm that come from inordinate joy in temporal goods. Do you see any of these traits in yourself? What damage is that doing to your relationship with God?

5. As you've grown closer to God, how have your own desires changed? What do you want now that you never used to want? What don't you want now that you used to want very much? How has that change in desires changed you and the way you live your life?

In Brief—St. Thérèse of Lisieux

Born—January 2, 1873 in Alençon, France.

Family—The youngest of nine children, born to Blessed Louis and Blessed Zélie Martin. Of the five children who survived childhood, four (including Thérèse) entered the Carmelite order, while one became a Visitation sister.

Lived—in Alençon and Lisieux, France until, at the age of fifteen, she entered the Carmelite Cloister in Lisieux. She remained there for the rest of her life.

Dreamed—of becoming a missionary. Although ill health, among other things, prevented her from becoming a Carmelite missionary, she corresponded faithfully with several missionary priests and prayed fervently for their success. Today, she is considered by the Church to be one of the main patron saints of all missionaries.

Found—"the little way" to God, a way marked by total trust in God and doing "little deeds" with "great love."

Wrote—*The Story of a Soul*, her spiritual autobiography written at the request of her religious superior (who was also her sister). Since her death, collections of her letters, poems, and final conversations with the Carmelite sisters have also been published.

Died—On September 30, 1897, at the age of twenty-four from tuberculosis.

Feast Day—October 1.

Key Terms

Temporal Goods
Natural Goods
Sensory Goods
Moral Goods
Supernatural Goods
Spiritual Goods

Chapter Six

THE STRUGGLE AGAINST SIN

Summary

God calls all men and women, both lay and religious, to holiness. He calls us, in the words of St. Francis de Sales, to the devout life. We can only answer that call, however, if we understand the nature of the devout life. All too often, the world confuses outward displays of piety with true devotion, failing to grasp the importance of inner transformation and love. That confusion not only undermines the living of the devout life, but also promotes false and even dangerous forms of spirituality.

Simply understanding the true nature of the devout life, however, isn't enough to make us holy. The devout life has to be lived, not just understood. And the first step towards living that life is rejecting serious sin. A soul can't truly pursue God without first determining to never knowingly and willingly commit grave moral offenses. Failing to reject mortal sin is choosing to remain cut off from grace—the food of the spiritual life.

After we reject serious sin, we next must reject the desire or affection for those sins. It's not enough to just stop sinning. To become holy, we also need to understand the horror of our sins.

We need to see them for the evil they are. Any affection for sin impedes spiritual progress.

Unlike mortal sins, venial sins don't cut us off from God's grace. They can, however, become serious impediments on the road to heaven if we don't take them seriously. Likewise, affection for venial sins or a lack of true contrition all too often open the door to more serious sins.

Guarding against scrupulosity on one hand and carelessness on the other the saints make an important distinction between *advertent* and *inadvertent* venial sins. Advertent venial sins are those we freely choose to commit after some reflection even though we know they are displeasing to God. Inadvertent venial sins are those that "just happen" without real reflection or considered choice. Teresa of Avila interpreted these as what the Scripture means when it says that "the just person falls seven times a day."

Questions for Comprehension
1. What according to St. Francis de Sales, characterizes true spirituality and devotion?

2. What does it mean to live the devout life?

3. What are two practices St. Francis recommends that can help souls reject serious sin?

4. What advice does St. Francis give for making a good confession?

5. What is the danger of nurturing affection for serious sin?

6. In order to free ourselves from affection for serious sin, what truths does St. Francis suggest we contemplate?

7. What is the two-edged sword with which St. Catherine of Siena says we should fight our spiritual battles?

8. What are the dangers of nurturing affection for venial sins?

9. Of what does St. Francis say perfection consists?

10. What do we need most in order to persevere in our struggle against sin?

Questions for Reflection

1. How do you think a false understanding of true devotion can lead a person away from God? Describe what that false understanding might look like.

2. In your own conversion, what serious sins did you have to first reject before you could pursue a more intimate relationship with Christ? Are there any serious sins you have not yet rejected? If so, why not? What damage do you think that is doing to your spiritual journey?

3. What venial sins do you struggle with the most? Why do you think these habits of sin have been so hard for you to break? How are these sins getting in the way of your relationship with God?

4. Look back at St. Francis de Sales' advice about the Sacrament of Confession. How much does your own practice of the Sacrament reflect that advice? What more can you do to take advantage of the graces offered in Confession?

5. Describe at least one occasion when God's grace enabled you to reject sin and an attachment for sin. How did that grace transform your heart as well as your actions?

In Brief—St. Francis de Sales

Born—August 21, 1567 in Thorens, a French city near the Swiss border.

Family—The son of aristocratic parents and the eldest of six brothers.

Tempted—to despair in his late teens by the theological disputes over predestination that raged at his college and throughout Europe. He was freed from that despair while praying before an image of the Blessed Virgin Mary. Immediately he made a private vow of consecration to her.

Served—as a priest for the Diocese of Geneva, and later as Bishop of Geneva.

Lived—for his entire ordained life in exile from his diocesan see in Geneva because Calvinists ruled it.

Worked—to win back souls to the Catholic Church, traveling throughout his diocese both as a priest and bishop preaching about the truths of the faith. He also established solid catechetical programs for the Catholic faithful, ensuring that they knew their faith well enough not to be swayed by Protestant arguments.

Wrote—the great treatise on lay spirituality, *Introduction to the Devout Life*, as well as numerous pamphlets defending the Catholic faith (now collected in one volume and published as *The Catholic Controversy*), and several other theological treatises still in print. Because of his vast literary output, he is now considered the patron saint of journalists and writers.

Died—September 28, 1622 at the age of fifty-five. His last word was a piece of advice given to a religious sister: "Humility."

Feast Day—January 24.

Key Terms

Mortal Sin
Venial Sin

Chapter Seven

THE IMPORTANCE OF PRAYER

Summary

The spiritual life is, first and foremost, a relationship. It is living in love and friendship with God. But, as with any relationship, that love and friendship don't just happen. Growing closer to God requires that we do the same things we do to grow closer to our friends and spouses: spend time together, listen, and share what we're thinking and feeling. In other words, growing closer to God requires prayer.

At its most basic, that's what prayer is—time spent listening to, talking to, and simply being with God. Prayer can be vocal—memorized or spontaneous words said aloud, alone or with others—or mental—thoughts and feelings wordlessly communicated. It can express joy, sorrow, gratitude, frustration, desire, contrition, anger, and faith. It can involve meditating on spiritual truths and biblical wisdom. It can begin with reading or by gazing upon holy images. And it can be carried out in the quiet of a church or in the noisy chaos of the office or home.

Regardless of where or how we pray, what matters most is that prayer be from the heart, a true act of communication and love, not simply the rote recitation of words and phrases, with the mind wandering far from the words uttered.

Through the centuries, the saints have offered a great deal of practical wisdom on how and when to pray. That wisdom always comes in the form of flexible suggestions, not hard and fast formulas. But when applied, those suggestions can bear great fruit. Included among them is St. Teresa of Avila's advice to always keep our focus on the One to whom we're speaking in prayer. Other saints, such as St. Francis de Sales, offer tips on when and where to pray, as well as how to combat distraction in prayer. St. Francis likewise lays out a pattern for our day, a rhythm of life to adopt that can help us stay close to the Lord in the midst of all our normal activities, while St. Bernard of Clairvaux teaches us how we can live a kind of prayerful solitude even in the midst of the busyness of life.

Again, different routines and habits will work better for some than for others. Nevertheless, the goal of prayer always remains the same: to feed our souls on that which they need to grow in love and virtue—namely a relationship with Christ.

Questions for Comprehension

1. How does St. Thérèse of Lisieux describe prayer?

2. According to St. Teresa of Avila, what determines the value of our prayers?

3. In your own words, list the six steps St. Francis de Sales suggests for a structured time of prayer?

4. Why, according to St. Francis, is it important to follow through on resolutions made in prayer?

5. According to St. Bernard of Clairvaux, from where do good thoughts in prayer come? From where do bad thoughts come?

6. If, against our will and despite our best efforts, temptations and distractions assault us while we're praying, what does St. Teresa advise us to do?

7. What is St. Francis's advice about when, where, and how long to pray?

8. In your own words, describe the plan St. Francis proposes to help us remember God throughout the day.

9. How, according to St. Bernard, can we be alone with God spiritually, even when we cannot be alone with Him physically?

10. What short prayer does St. Bernard recommend we pray as often as possible in order to stay close to God at all times?

Questions for Reflection

1. Describe your own prayer life. How often do you pray? Where do you pray? When do you pray? To what type of prayer do you devote the most time—mental or vocal?

2. How closely does your prayer life—the how, where, when, and what—reflect the advice of saints such as Teresa, Francis, and Bernard? What are the weaknesses in your prayer life? What are the strengths?

3. When you pray, how attentive are you to the one to whom you're praying? When do you find you're the most attentive? The least? What steps can you take to increase your attentiveness in prayer?

4. Is distraction a problem for you when you pray? What have you done to combat this problem? What more do you think you could do?

5. List the obstacles that most frequently get in the way of you spending as much time in prayer as you would like. What are some steps you can take to overcome these obstacles?

In Brief—St. Teresa of Avila

Born—March 28, 1515 in Avila, Spain.

Family—One of eleven children born to a wealthy Spanish knight, who was himself the son of a Jewish convert.

Educated—as a teenager by a religious order. Preferring convent life to her father's home or marriage, she entered the Carmelite order against her father's wishes at the age of twenty.

Combated—worldliness and laxity within the Carmelite order. Teresa protested against the vanity and flirtations of nuns, as well as the preferences given to wealthy sisters, and the disregard for both poverty and prayer.

Misunderstood—by just about everyone. Her friends and confessors were often suspicious of the communications she received from the Lord. The Carmelite order opposed her reforms. Her fellow sisters threatened to report her to the Inquisition, and a princess who had asked her to found a convent actually did report her. The publication of her books was held up for many years while the Inquisition examined them before eventually approving them. To top it all off, the papal nuncio described her as a "restless disobedient gadabout who has gone about teaching as though she were a professor."

Founded—the Discalced Carmelites with St. John of the Cross. By the time of her death, there were seventeen reformed monasteries for women and ten reformed monasteries for men.

Wrote—her autobiography, *The Life of St. Theresa of Jesus*, as well as *The Way of Perfection*, *The Interior Castle*, and several smaller theological treatises and reflections.

Died—in 1582 at the age of sixty-seven.

Feast Day—October 15.

Key Terms

Contemplative Prayer
Lectio Divina
Meditation
Mental Prayer
Vocal Prayer

Chapter Eight

TEMPTATIONS AND TRIALS

Summary

On every spiritual journey, temptations and trials present themselves. Those temptations and trials can delay, obstruct, or even end our journey to God. But, if responded to correctly, they can also spur us on to greater devotion, produce greater faith, and lead us ever closer to holiness.

In the beginning of our journey, temptations to excessive devotion, misplaced priorities, and a failure to see life from an eternal perspective are among the most common obstacles we encounter. Our own human weakness likewise presents the devil with countless opportunities to distract us and dissuade us from following God. In order to resist and overcome these temptations, we need to know our own sins and weaknesses, as well as God's mercy and strength.

Overcoming temptation also requires that we focus on both the immediate challenges to growth and the opportunities for grace that God presents to us each and every day. When done with a desire to please God, small sacrifices and small acts of love can become powerful means of resisting temptation and growing in holiness.

Overcoming temptation, however, can begin before temptations come. Avoiding near occasions of sin will help us to protect ourselves from temptations that we might not otherwise have the strength to resist. When temptations do come, the most important moment for resistance is when they first appear. The best thing we can do at that moment is run to the Cross of Christ and ask for His assistance.

It's also important to recognize that the temptations themselves are not the problem. The problem is our response. No matter how holy we become, temptations to sin will always appear. In fact, some of the greatest temptations were experienced by the greatest of saints. But they struggled against the temptation, calling on God for help, and grew in faith accordingly. They understood that temptation is not the same as sin. It's not a sin to experience temptation, but rather to entertain temptation, take pleasure in temptation, or succumb to temptation.

Trials, as well as temptations, make an appearance on every soul's journey to God. One of the most common of these trials is dryness in prayer. Although there are various reasons (and various remedies) for this dryness, all of us will experience this trial at one point or another. Discerning the remedy for the dryness begins with discerning its cause. Like temptation, however, this trial, when properly responded to, can become a great occasion for growing in faith, hope, and love.

Questions for Comprehension

1. In your own words, describe the three temptations that, according to St. Teresa of Avila, occur most frequently during the early stages of a person's spiritual journey.

2. What remedies do St. Teresa and St. Francis de Sales specifically propose for each of those three temptations.

3. Why is it important to have both self-knowledge and an awareness of God's mercy?

4. Describe St. Thérèse of Lisieux's "little way." What are some specific ways she lived this "little way"?

5. According to St. Francis, what dangers can come from seeking merely "good feelings" from prayer?

6. List the three steps of temptation that St. Francis identifies. Why is the most crucial step the second one?

7. Why is it so important to avoid near occasions of sin?

8. List at least four other things that can help you overcome temptations to sin.

9. What are the three main causes of dryness in prayer? What is the remedy recommended for each of the different causes?

10. Why does God sometimes allow us to feel dryness in prayer? What good can He bring from such a trial?

Questions for Reflection
1. List two or three practical ways you can imitate St. Thérèse's "little way." How do you think that "little way" will help you persevere through trials and temptations?

2. What is your first response when a serious temptation presents itself? Is that how you should respond? If not, what should you do? Be specific.

3. What are some near occasions of sin that you have learned to avoid? What are some near occasions of sin that you still need to learn to avoid? Why do you think you have continued to put yourself in those situations? What harm is that doing to you?

4. Evaluate the current state of your prayer life. Are you experiencing any dryness? If so, what do you think the source of that dryness is?

5. How much do you rely on "good feelings" or spiritual consolations? How do you think your relationship with God would change in the absence of those good feelings and consolations?

In Brief—St. John of the Cross

Born—near Avila, Spain in 1542.

Family—The son of a young aristocrat who left his family and wealth to marry the daughter of a poor weaver. John was the youngest of three boys who, after the death of their father when John was only two years old, struggled to make ends meet.

Studied—at a school run by the Jesuits, thanks to the generosity of his uncle, a priest. In his spare time, John earned money for his family by working at a hospital.

Entered—the Carmelite order, but remained a Carmelite and was ordained a priest only after St. Teresa of Avila persuaded him not to leave the Carmelites for the Carthusians (one of the strictest contemplative monastic orders).

Imprisoned—for nine months by his own order in a cell barely as big as his body and beaten by those same brothers, thrice weekly. The reason? His partnership with Teresa of Avila in founding houses of reformed or "discalced" Carmelites.

Wrote—what are widely considered the greatest mystical treatises of all time, including *The Dark Night of the Soul, Spiritual Canticle, Ascent of Mt. Carmel* and *Living Flame of Love*.

Influenced—modern day saints such as St. Thérèse of Lisieux (who kept one of his books by her bedside during her dying days), and modern day philosophers and thinkers such as Hans urs von Balthasar, Thomas Merton, Jacques Maritain, and Pope John Paul II, who wrote his dissertation on St. John.

Died—December 14, 1591 from an infection in his leg.

Feast Day—December 14.

Key Terms

Active Night of the Senses
Dark Night of the Senses

Chapter Nine

A CERTAIN STABILITY

Summary

When we are about to enter the beginning of the illuminative stage (or what St. Teresa of Avila describes as moving from the third mansion to the fourth mansion), our lives bear a marked resemblance to the stereotypical image of the "good Catholic." We practice virtue in our personal and professional lives; we pray regularly and fast when we ought; we give generously and are not consumed by the things of the world.

For lay people, as well as religious, this stage doesn't have to be the end of our spiritual journey. We can progress much farther, all the way to deep spiritual union with God. But, for many, it is the end. Our progress towards God comes to a halt here, usually because of lack of knowledge or lack of desire.

In order to become holy—truly holy—two kinds of knowledge are necessary: knowledge of self and knowledge of God. Knowledge of self involves an understanding of both the dignity and beauty of man and the ugliness of sin. Knowledge of God requires a recognition of His incredible love and mercy. Together, those two types of knowledge enable us to move forwards towards God, hopeful and unafraid.

Desire for holiness, desire for God, is also a prerequisite for achieving spiritual union. It's never enough to simply know progress in holiness is possible. We also must want it with all our hearts. We can't, however, produce that desire on our own. True desire is a gift of the Holy Spirit. The Holy Spirit draws us towards God, transforms our minds and wills, and increases our knowledge and love of God. Accordingly, the saints urge us to call upon the Holy Spirit again and again, to ask for His help and the gifts that are His to give.

If we want to reach the end of our spiritual journey, our prayer should always be "Come Holy Spirit, Come."

Questions for Comprehension

1. List the characteristics that St. Teresa of Avila attributes to souls in the third stage (or third mansion) of the spiritual journey.

2. How does St. Teresa describe a soul untainted by mortal sin? How does that image compare to her description of a soul in the grips of sin?

3. According to St. Bernard, where is the true home of God? What are the attributes of this home?

4. What is the danger of possessing self-knowledge without also possessing knowledge of God? What does God tell St. Catherine of Siena the devil will attempt to do with our awareness of our own sinfulness?

5. What biblical evidence suggests that progress in the spiritual life is possible? In your own words, summarize at least two Scriptural passages cited in this chapter that tell us holiness is an attainable goal.

6. What is one of the ways God increases our desire for Him?

7. Does our desire for God end when we reach the end of our spiritual journey? According to St. Bernard of Clairvaux, why or why not?

8. When we lack a strong desire for God, what should we do? What will happen when we do that?

9. Even if our desire for God is not great at any given moment, how can we know if God is still at work in our life?

10. What is the "kiss" of God? What does this "kiss" accomplish? How does that "kiss" resemble St. John of the Cross's idea of the twofold dimension of contemplation?

Questions for Reflection

1. Do you ever find yourself becoming complacent about your relationship with God? What are the dangers inherent in that way of thinking?

2. Over the course of your life, how have you come to know yourself better? Who or what has helped you attain self-knowledge? What have been the most startling things you've learned about yourself?

3. Who or what has proven the most helpful in bringing you to a greater knowledge of God? As your knowledge of God has grown, how has your relationship with Him changed?

4. How frequently does your desire for God waver? What do you think is the cause of that wavering? When it happens, what is your response? Does you response help or hurt the situation? What do you think your response should be?

In Brief—Bernard of Clairvaux

Born—In 1090 near Dijon, France.

Family—The third of seven children born to Blessed Tescelin, Lord of Fontaies, and Blessed Aleth of Montbard. Five of Bernard's siblings were also declared "blessed" by the Church.

Entered—the austere Cistercian order in 1112, along with thirty other young nobleman, including his uncle and brothers whom he had persuaded to enter with him.

Refused—multiple bishoprics, preferring instead the life of abbot and preacher.

Preached—the Second Crusade throughout France and Germany at the request of Pope Eugene III. Thousands of men responded with enthusiasm to his call to take back the Holy Land from Muslims. When the crusade failed, in part perhaps because of the sins of the Crusaders, many blamed Bernard, who emerged from the controversy faithful to his mission in the Church.

Healed—the Great Schism that followed the death of Pope Honorius II in 1130. With two men both claiming the papacy, the Church's bishops asked Bernard to decide who was the legitimate pope. Bernard chose Pope Innocent II, and his decision was accepted by the ruling powers of Europe.

Wrote—hundreds of homilies, letters, and theological treatises, including his most famous on the "Song of Songs."

Died—on August 20, 1153.

Feast Day—August 20.

Key Terms

Self-Knowledge
Despair
Kiss of God

Chapter Ten

GROWING IN FREEDOM

Summary

In order to draw us to Him, God filled the world with people, pleasures, and created things—good and beautiful works of His hands. He intended those works to help us on our journey to Him. They were designed to teach us about God, point the way to God, and inspire us to move towards God. But then our first parents fell from grace. Now, as a result, the very people and things God designed to draw us towards Him often have just the opposite effect. They can become obstacles, not helps, to holiness. We invest our hearts in them, not God, and look to them for happiness, fulfillment, and even salvation. We make idols for ourselves and lose our way.

Accordingly, progress in the spiritual life requires a growing detachment from the goods of this world. We must let go of our disordered desires and put God first. That doesn't mean we have to stop loving the things of the world. Rather, by reordering our loves and seeking happiness the way God intended us to seek it, we are in fact able to love those things even more—with greater freedom and with greater understanding.

One of the most basic things we need to detach from is an inordinate desire for money and possessions. While God doesn't call all Christians to live in poverty, He does call all Christians to be "poor in spirit"—to give freely, to not set our hearts on accumulating more possessions, and to never seek gain at another's expense. He also calls Christians to detach themselves from sensual pleasures, asking even married Christians to embrace the virtue of chastity. Ultimately, chastity means living out the Church's teachings on sexuality according to our state in life, and never letting our sexual desires trump fidelity or charity.

Perhaps the most difficult love from which we must detach ourselves is love of self—pride. Pride blinds us to our own failings and tempts us into believing that our salvation will result from our own merits and good works. That pride must be broken and humility embraced if we are to grow closer to God. Through accepting trials and misfortunes, cultivating patience, and letting go of our desire for respect and admiration, we can acquire the virtues we need to renounce pride and rightly reorder our loves and desires.

Questions for Comprehension

1. According to St. John of the Cross, what are the signs of true detachment from money and possessions?

2. What are the spiritual ramifications of giving our hearts to money, possessions, and things?

3. What advice does St. Francis de Sales give about how to practice chastity?

4. Why, according to St. Bernard of Clairvaux, is pride the beginning of all sin?

5. How does pride obscure our understanding of salvation?

6. How, according to St. Bernard, should we view the merits we possess?

7. What are some of the ways we can consciously choose to humble ourselves? How will doing that help us overcome pride and self-love?

8. How can illness and physical suffering become a means of overcoming pride?

9. What is the connection between pride and impatience?

10. To what four areas did St. Francis de Sales say our obedience to God's will should extend? How can practicing obedience help us grow in humility?

Questions for Reflection

1. Look back at St. Francis's indicators for discerning a spirit of detachment or poverty. Using those indicators as a guide, how attached are you to money and material possessions? What are two or three practical things you can do to grow less attached to those things?

2. Our attachment to sensual pleasure can be expressed in both thought and action. Is either form of attachment a struggle for you? If so, explain. How can you start putting the advice the saints give about detachment from sensual pleasures into practice?

3. Think back to a time when you made a mistake or committed a sin and were justly criticized. Describe the situation. How

did you react? Were there any traces of pride in that reaction? In order to cultivate humility, how should you react in similar situations in the future?

4. What occasions for practicing patience and humility exist right now in your life? Is there any way you can change your attitude or behavior to better embrace those opportunities? If so, how?

5. To whom, if anyone, are you obedient? Does obedience come easily for you or is it a struggle? Why do you think that is? Is there someone you can envision yourself submitting to on spiritual matters, and if so, what could the benefits of such a relationship be?

More About—Gifts of the Holy Spirit

Nobody likes to put a number on the gifts the Holy Spirit can give, but, based on Scripture alone, there are, at minimum, thirty such gifts.

First, there are the Isaian gifts enumerated in Isaiah 11:2–3: wisdom, understanding, counsel, fortitude (courage and endurance), knowledge, piety, and fear of the Lord.

Then there are the charismatic gifts outlined by Paul in 1 Corinthians 12:4–10: wisdom, knowledge, discerning of spirits, speaking in tongues, interpretation of tongues, prophecy, faith, working of miracles, and healing. Additional gifts are listed in Romans 12:6-8: prophecy, ministry, teaching, exhortation, giving, leading, and showing compassion through works of mercy.

Then there are the apostolic gifts named in Ephesians 4:11. These are the leadership gifts of apostles, prophets, evangelists, pastors, and teachers.

Lastly, marriage and celibacy are listed as gifts in 1 Corinthians 7:7.

Regardless of where these gifts fall on the various lists, they all share one thing in common: they are all gifts which the Holy Spirit dispenses for our good and the good of the Church. Scripture also makes it clear that we're never to compare our gifts with those of another. As Christians, we each possess different gifts in different ways and measures, and are all called to use and cultivate those gifts in the service of others. In giving what has been given to us, God is glorified.

Key Terms

Poverty of Spirit

Chapter Eleven

GROWING IN LOVE

Summary

Growing in holiness is really about growing in love—love of God and love of neighbor. The more we love, the more closely we resemble God, who is love.

Although our love for God usually begins in fear—in a desire to escape damnation and receive salvation—it should gradually progress, developing first into a love that seeks to know and please the Lord, then, eventually, into a deep, lasting filial love that seeks nothing for itself. This type of love marks a pure, abiding union with Christ.

As we grow in love of God, we should, at the same time, grow in love of our neighbors. Broadly speaking, this means we should practice sincere Christian charity to friends and strangers alike, loving them without expecting anything in return. It also means we should cultivate strong, healthy Christian friendships. Although it's important to root out selfish and impure motives from our love, God made us to live in friendship with one another, and friendships can help us on our journey towards God. Jesus Himself had these types of close friendships, as did many of the saints.

Importantly, these healthy and holy relationships don't end when we leave this world: in eternity, the bonds between souls only grow stronger. Both the angels and saints in heaven love the souls on earth and in purgatory, and they express their friendship with us through their prayers.

Marriage is a special form of Christian friendship. Good Christian marriages are marked by sincere affection, fidelity, open communication, and a deep desire for the good of the other. When properly understood and exercised, married sexuality can deepen the friendship and communion of persons, as well as bring forth new life. Although this sexuality can be abused, it is, when used as God intended, a good, which we should respect as a holy mystery.

Questions for Comprehension

1. How does St. Catherine of Siena describe the soul's growth in love? What images does she use for each stage? Describe how those images correlate to each stage in the process.

2. How does St. Bernard describe "pure love"?

3. What, according to St. Bernard and St. Catherine, are some of the actions which love of neighbor requires?

4. How, according to St. Catherine, can we know if our love for another is selfish?

5. What is the danger of intimate friendship between men and women who are not married?

6. Why does St. Francis encourage Christians to only pursue close friendships with other Christians? Why are such friendships between Christians "excellent"?

7. Why does St. Francis say "particular friendships" are necessary for lay people, but potentially dangerous for religious?

8. What does St. Francis say are the three effects of true married love?

9. In your own words, sum up the analogy St. Francis makes between food and married, sexual love.

10. Based upon what you read in this chapter, list at least three ways that Christian couples can pervert married love and impair the friendship they should enjoy with one another.

Questions for Reflection

1. On what is your love of God based? How is this reflected in your actions?

2. In what ways do you regularly fail to obey the command, "Love your neighbor"? What do you think is the reason for your failing? What are some specific steps you can take to remedy the situation?

3. Describe a friendship that has led you closer to Christ. Who is the friend? How long have you known this person? In what way has this friendship brought you closer to holiness?

4. Friendships can lead us away from Christ, as well as to him. Have you ever had a friend who proved spiritually "dangerous"? What was the source of that danger? What attracted you to the friendship to begin with? What have you learned from that experience?

5. If you are single and open to being married or already married, what are some practical things you can do now that will contribute to authentic love and Christian friendship between you and your (present or future) spouse?

More About—The Four Loves

In English, there is only one word for love. In ancient Greek, however, there were four: *storge, philia, eros,* and *agape.* Together, those four words express the spectrum of loves we can and should experience.

Storge essentially means "affection." It describes a love bred through familiarity, such as that which we feel for our family members and neighbors, or even for our dog.

Philia describes the love shared between two friends. It is a love based on respect and common interests.

Eros is passion, the feelings of admiration, longing, and sexual desire felt by two people "in love" with one another.

Agape is charity, the greatest of the loves and a specifically Christian virtue. All the other loves are most fully realized when they are infused with charity, where God is loved above all and the neighbor is loved selflessly, for that soul's own sake and without thought of gain. While the first three loves are considered "natural loves," charity is a supernatural love, made possible only by God's grace, *but it can inform and shape the other loves as well.*

Key Terms

Filial Love

Slavish Fear

Chapter Twelve

GROWING IN PRAYER

Summary

All prayer is communion with God. But, as we progress in the Christian life, our prayers take on a new intensity and depth. The difference between prayer early in our journey and late in our journey is generally a difference of degree—the degree to which we are absorbed in the Lord.

In the beginning, we do most of the work in prayer. It takes effort to quiet our minds and hearts, to focus on God, and to speak with Him. But, through meditating on the life of Christ, the truths of salvation history, and the teachings of the faith, we can—at least to some degree—succeed in that effort. Even when our minds wander and we have no desire for meditating, the mere act of attempting to pray can bear fruit.

Over time, however, if we persist in prayer despite these seeming obstacles, quieting our souls and listening to God becomes easier. We're more able to think of the Lord and pay attention to Him. We have a heightened awareness of His presence, and, eventually, we find that we do less work and He does more. This type of prayer is often described as infused recollection or contemplation.

As with prayer in general, there are different degrees of contemplative prayer. There is contemplative prayer where our wills are turned to God, even though our thoughts, memories, and imagination may wander. And there is contemplative prayer where our wills, as well as all our other faculties are focused on God. This type of contemplative prayer is sometimes called "the prayer of union," when at times our whole being can become absorbed in the Lord. At times we can even for short periods lose our awareness of time, physical sensation, and the world around us.

It's important to remember that growing in prayer is not about perfecting this or that technique. It's about growing in relationship with the Lord, and allowing Him to work in us so that our wills can be more closely united with His. That union of wills, not the experience of contemplation or consolation, is what God is after. He wants to bring us to the point where we perfectly love Him and perfectly love our neighbor. He can accomplish that even in souls to whom He never grants the prayer of deepest union. It's His mercy, and nothing else, that enables us to become holy. Prayer is simply a way (albeit an important way) of opening ourselves up to receiving that mercy.

Questions for Comprehension

1. Why, even when we are distracted in prayer, can our efforts to pray still bear fruit?

2. What is "acquired recollection"? How, specifically, can it be achieved?

3. How does acquired recollection differ from "infused recollection"? List some of the characteristics that accompany infused recollection.

4. According to St. Teresa of Avila and St. Bernard of Clairvaux, what are some of the steps we can take to make ourselves more disposed to receiving the gift of infused recollection or contemplation?

5. Define contemplation.

6. What benefits did St. Bernard say that he reaped from his "visits" with the Lord?

7. How, according to St. Teresa, can a soul know if it has experienced the prayer of union?

8. What does God make possible through the experience of union in prayer?

9. How does St. Teresa understand the obstacles we encounter on our journey to God?

Questions for Reflection

1. When you are distracted or uninterested in praying, do you still continue to pray? Why or why not? If at times you have persisted, what benefits have come from doing that?

2. Reflect upon the different levels of prayer outlined in this chapter. Which levels have you experienced? How has God used those experiences to draw you closer to Him?

3. The depth of our prayer life can vary from week to week, month to month, and year to year. Under what circumstances have you found that your prayer life has flourished? What can cause it to suffer?

4. Why do you pray? In other words, what are you most often seeking when you go to God in prayer? Do you seek consolations or the granting of favors? If so, what are the dangers of that kind of motivation?

5. How could taking St. Thérèse of Lisieux's "shortcut" to God deepen your experience of prayer?

More About—Spending Time with God

How can we find time to spend with God in the midst of our busy lives? By starting small and looking for little moments to be with Him.

Before you even get out of bed in the morning, take five minutes to thank God for the day and give all of its challenges and joys back to Him by making a morning offering. Then, in the car, turn off the radio and begin your drive to work or school by talking with Him. It can also help to keep a Rosary in your pocket or purse so that you can pray a decade or a Divine Mercy Chaplet while waiting in line at the grocery store or sitting in the doctor's office. If you regularly drive or walk past a Church, say a quick prayer as you go by. Even better, once a day stop the car and pop in for a quick five-minute visit before the tabernacle.

These small moments of prayer are important, but they're also never enough. We need quiet hours, not just quiet minutes, with God. If you can, spend the first thirty to sixty minutes of your day in the Lord's presence, perhaps saying the Rosary, praying the Morning Office (or the abbreviated version found in the publication, *Magnificat*), reading Scripture or some other spiritual work, or simply going over your day with Him. Or just being with Him. Do the same before you fall asleep at night: look back on the day with Him, make an examination of conscience, and give thanks and praise for the events that unfolded.

Lastly, if your parish has Eucharistic adoration, make a commitment to spend at least one hour there every week. Put the appointment on your calendar, just as you would with any other appointment, and keep it faithfully. In those quiet hours with Him, where no phones are ringing or emails pinging, you'll be able to live the words of the psalm: "Be still and know that I am God."

Key Terms

Recollection
Contemplation
Prayer of Quiet
Sleep of Faculties
Prayer of Union

Chapter Thirteen

HELP FROM HEAVEN

Summary

The work of transformation doesn't always proceed at a regular pace. At times, God accelerates the process, helping us draw nearer to Him through very specific gifts of grace. These gifts prepare us for deeper union with the Lord. Not every soul will experience these gifts—they aren't a necessary part of the journey—but when responded to correctly, they can be an important help in the pursuit of holiness.

Sometimes, we experience these gifts of grace as a desire for greater solitude—more "alone time" with the Lord. At other times, we experience them as "touches" or "wounds" in the soul that fill us with a deep, abiding, and all-consuming desire for God. These "wounds" not only make us willing to accept suffering, but actually cause us to desire trials and opportunities for renunciation and mortification.

To some, God also offers the graces of locutions, audible or inaudible words from Him that give direction, inspiration, consolation, or even bring about an immediate change in a person's soul. The real benefit of locutions, however, comes when they direct our attention not to the form of the locution, but rather to God Himself.

The same can be said of visions. Regardless of whether the vision takes on a visible bodily form or whether it remains a vision only in the mind's eye, the purpose of any true vision is to deepen our trust in and love for God. To focus too much on the vision or to see it as a particular sign of God's favor can ultimately distract us from recognizing its true purpose. It can also blind us to our true spiritual poverty.

Regardless of which gifts of grace God bestows on us, we should never seek these consolations and only rarely rely on them when they are received. Words of prophecy can be difficult to understand, and too much focus on supernatural guidance can cause us to ignore the most common guidance God gives—guidance though reason, common sense, and trusted advisors. It can also lead us to forget that in this world, we "walk by faith, not by sight" (2 Cor. 5:7).

Questions for Comprehension

1. What are two or three of the ways the saints describe the "wounds" of love God gives to certain souls?

2. What are the fruits of authentic "wounds of love?" How can these be differentiated from the imitation "wounds of love" that the devil can inflict?

3. List and define the four different types of locutions that God can use to communicate to a soul.

4. How does St. John of the Cross say we should respond to these locutions? What reason does he give for that recommendation?

5. What particular danger is associated with successive locutions?

6. List and define the three types of visions a soul can experience.

7. Why does St. John of the Cross say that a soul doesn't need to focus on certain types of visions, even if they are authentic?

8. Why is it important for someone who is experiencing locutions or visions to seek out a good spiritual director or confessor?

9. What are some of the characteristics of authentic visions or insights? What are the characteristics of visions or insights produced by the devil?

10. From where, besides visions and locutions, should we look to receive wisdom from God?

Questions for Reflection

1. Has God ever called you to spend more time alone with Him? Were you able to answer that call? If not, why? What are some practical ways you can make more room in your life for time alone with God?

2. What types of problems do you think could arise from a person valuing locutions more than reason, common sense, the teachings of the Church, and trusted advisors? Have you ever personally experienced any of those problems?

3. Do you have a spiritual director? If so, how have you benefited from his advice? If not, do you know anyone you could ask to be your spiritual director? If not, do you have a spiritual friend

that you can share with? How do you think you could benefit from that friend's support and guidance?

4. How frequently do you ask God for signs and spiritual consolations? If very frequently, why? For what should you be asking?

5. Who are the people through whom God most often speaks to you? How has their witness, counsel, or criticism helped you on your journey to God?

More About—Helpers from Heaven

Who is smarter than Einstein, stronger than Superman, and created specifically to serve you?

Your guardian angel.

According to the *Catechism of the Catholic Church* (no. 328–349), all angels, guardian angels included, are pure spirits. They all have intelligence and will. They all are personal and immortal. And the glory of every angel surpasses that of all visible creatures.

All angels, however, are not the same. There are angels and archangels, seraphim and cherubim, and an entire hierarchy of other angels who all carry out different tasks. Some have the specific task of worshipping before God's throne. Others are messengers to man from God. Others still have tasks that Scripture and Tradition have not revealed.

What Scripture has revealed though, is that each of us has a guardian angel, created by God to serve us, and who is entrusted with the task of helping us get to heaven (Mt. 18:10). We can and should call on our angel day and night for help, wisdom, and guidance, just as we would with any trusted friend. We also can and should thank him for all the help, known and unknown, that he gives us each day. Even when we see no visions and hear no locutions, help from heaven is always coming our way thanks to our guardian angel.

Key Terms

Wounds of Love
Pure Contemplation
Active Night of the Spirit

Chapter Fourteen

A DEEPER PURIFICATION

Summary

Early on in our journey to God, we experience trials and sufferings that help purify us of our sinful habits and inordinate attachments. But the effects of that purification only go so far. Sin is deeply rooted in human nature and has damaged us to the very core of our beings. Accordingly, before we can enjoy full union with God the purification must go deeper.

The need for deeper purification is evident in how sin can sometimes twist even our spiritual aspirations. Sin and its effects can also lead us to choose the wrong spiritual disciplines at the wrong time, as well as to sin against our friends and family members in any number of ways.

Although, we can attempt to purify ourselves of these sins and their effects, our own efforts can only accomplish so much. God must do the rest. And to do that, He uses both exterior and interior trials. These trials aren't optional. They are a necessary part of the spiritual journey, and if purification doesn't happen on earth, it then must happen in purgatory.

When it comes to exterior trials, God uses illness and pain, persecution, poverty, human misunderstandings, rejection, and other forms of suffering to purify our hearts and lead us to deeper trust in Him. Interior trials can affect us even more deeply. These may consist of a feeling of abandonment by God, prolonged and deep aridity in prayer, and a profound awareness of our brokenness and sinfulness. Although God feels absent during this time, this kind of trial is, in fact, a work of God in the soul. Even when we can't perceive His presence and receive no sign of consolation, He is still there, guiding us and giving us the strength to endure.

During this "dark night of the spirit" the fallen parts of our human nature undergo a type of crucifixion. Our suffering unites us to Christ, and as we die to ourselves, our capacity to love God grows. When the time of this purification comes to an end, the Lord has brought us to a deeper union which has increased our capacity to love God and others as we ought, and to experience His love.

Questions for Comprehension
1. List each of the capital sins. For each, give one example of how that particular sin can disguise itself in spiritual trappings.

2. What is the difference between the "active night of the spirit" and the "passive night of the spirit"?

3. Why is it better for us that this deeper stage of purification takes place in this life, not the next, and that it takes place as soon as possible?

4. Why do so many of the Church Doctors use the image of fire to describe this time of purification? In your own words, explain the metaphor that St. John of the Cross uses to illustrate the process of purification.

5. How, according to St. Teresa of Avila, can we endure the trials that God sends our way? Is there any remedy for them? If so, what?

6. Although we can't perceive it, what does St. John say God is actually doing during the dark night? Why can we not perceive this?

7. Where in Scripture do we find evidence of the existence of the dark night of the spirit and our need for purification? Give at least three examples.

8. What, according to St. John, must be crucified or "annihilated" in the dark night of the spirit?

9. According to St. John, how does the dark night of the spirit affect our intellect, will, and memory?

10. What is promised to those who pass through the dark night of the spirit?

Questions for Reflection

1. St. Augustine famously prayed, "Lord make me chaste, but not yet." After reading this chapter, do you find yourself praying, "Lord make me holy, but not yet"? If so, why do you think that is? What, if anything, can you do to change that reaction?

2. Does the need for this type of purification change your understanding of the nature of original sin? If so, how?

3. Reflect back upon the ways that sin can work its way into the practice of the faith. Which of these sins have affected your own spiritual journey? Which of these sins are you currently guilty of committing?

4. Think back to a time when God permitted an exterior or interior trial to afflict you. Describe the situation. How did you respond to it? How did the trial change you? Did it bring you closer to God? If so, why do you think that is?

5. Describe someone you know who has endured great suffering without losing faith in God. What have you learned from this person? Have you been encouraged to endure your own trials? How can meditating on the words of 1 Corinthians 10:13 increase our confidence in God's providential wisdom and love in our regard?

More About—Purgatory

"All who die in God's grace and friendship, but still imperfectly purified, are indeed assured of their eternal salvation; but after death they undergo purification, so as to achieve the holiness necessary to enter the joy of heaven.

"The Church gives the name *Purgatory* to this final purification of the elect, which is entirely different from the punishment of the damned [Cf. Council of Florence (1439): DS 1304; Council of Trent (1563): DS 1820; (1547): 1580; see also Benedict XII, *Benedictus Deus* (1336): DS 1000]. The Church formulated her doctrine of faith on Purgatory especially at the Councils of Florence and Trent. The tradition of the Church, by reference to certain texts of Scripture, speaks of a cleansing fire [Cf. 1 Cor 3:15; 1 Pet 1:7]. . . .

"This teaching is also based on the practice of prayer for the dead, already mentioned in Sacred Scripture: 'Therefore [Judas Maccabeus] made atonement for the dead, that they might be delivered from their sin' [2 Macc 12:46]. From the beginning the Church has honored the memory of the dead and offered prayers in suffrage for them, above all the Eucharistic sacrifice, so that, thus purified, they may attain the beatific vision of God [Cf. Council of Lyons II (1274): DS 856]. The Church also commends almsgiving, indulgences, and works of penance undertaken on behalf of the dead" (*The Catechism of the Catholic Church*, paragraphs 1030–1032).

Key Terms ————————————————————————————————

The Dark Night of the Spirit

Chapter Fifteen

DEEP UNION

Summary

If we continue on in faith, in virtue, in love, and in the patient endurance of all suffering, we enter, by God's grace, into a deep union with Him. In this life, that union occurs in two phases: what the mystics describe as spiritual betrothal and spiritual marriage.

Spiritual betrothal, like any engagement, indicates that full union—a spiritual marriage—will indeed occur if we remain faithful and cooperate with God's grace at work in our soul. During this time of betrothal, we enjoy an abiding and attentive relationship with the Lord, a relationship typically marked by a sense of tranquility in the soul and frequent communication with God. By the time we reach this stage, God has purified our souls of most sins. Nevertheless, traces of our fallen nature still manifest themselves in small defects and attachments to the goods of the world or goods of the spirit. Those imperfections become the source of some of the suffering experienced during the time of spiritual betrothal. We also suffer during this stage when the Lord withdraws our experience of His presence, love and favor, perhaps permitting an increase of trials and temptations.

Once we enter into spiritual marriage, however, those small imperfections and attachments are substantially left behind, and we're able to enjoy God's presence within us rather constantly. To reach this state is to enjoy a powerful and personal relationship with the Lord. Our entire being is, in a sense, fused into His, and His life becomes an almost inextricable part of our own life. Nevertheless, most of the saints and doctors agree that even if we achieve this state of union, we can still fall into sin, turn our backs on the Lord, and lose our salvation if we begin to become careless and fall prey to subtle temptations to pride or confidence in our own virtue.

For those who do persevere in faith and never lose the grace of spiritual marriage, however, one final step in the journey remains—death. Only after this life is over, can we see God as He is and enjoy the blessings of the beatific vision. Even the holiest of souls can only bear so much light while they remain in the world. On earth, we can see only so much of God, and His final revelation of Himself awaits the day when He welcomes us into heaven.

Questions for Comprehension

1. What are the different ways the moment of spiritual betrothal can be experienced?

2. Describe the imperfections in the intellect and will that St. John says can still remain in a soul "betrothed" to the Lord.

3. How did those imperfections manifest themselves in the life of St. Thérèse of Liseux?

4. According to St. Bernard, what can happen at the moment of death that frees the soul from spiritual imperfections and enables it to enter into a spiritual marriage?

5. What is the difference between a spiritual betrothal and a spiritual marriage?

6. How, according to Pope Benedict XVI, is the Blessed Virgin Mary the perfect model of a soul in the state of spiritual marriage?

7. What metaphors do St. John and St. Bernard use to describe spiritual marriage?

8. What, according to St. Bernard, does a soul contemplating Christ's face in heaven desire? What does such a soul lack? How does this contemplation differ from contemplation of Him on earth?

9. Why, according to most saints and doctors, can souls in the unitive state still lose their salvation?

10. What does St. Bernard advise such souls to do in order to prevent themselves from turning away from Christ.

Questions for Reflection

1. How does the varied pace at which the different doctors proceeded to union with God help you understand the progression of your own spiritual journey?

2. What does St. Thérèse's struggle with imperfections and attachments, even during the time of her spiritual betrothal, tell you about the primacy of grace in the soul's movement towards God?

3. Look back at your answer to question number ten above. How is St. Bernard's advice helpful even for souls who have not yet entered the unitive stage?

More about—The *Magnificat*

After Mary received the Good News that she would bear the Son of God, she left Nazareth to visit her cousin Elizabeth. When Mary entered her cousin's house, Elizabeth greeted her with the words: "Blessed are you among women, and blessed is the fruit of your womb. And why is this granted me, that the mother of my Lord, should come to me?"

Mary's response to those words was a song of praise for God's saving plan. That song is the prayer we call the *Magnificat*.

The *Magnificat* is described by the *Catechism* as "the song of both the Mother of God and the Church" (no. 2619). It is a prayer that perfectly expresses the miracles wrought in a soul by God's great grace. And it is a prayer that all Christians can claim as their own.

My soul proclaims the greatness of the Lord,
my spirit rejoices in God my Savior;
for He has looked with favor on His lowly servant.
From this day all generations shall call me blessed.
The Almighty has done great things for me,
and holy is His Name.
He has mercy on those who fear Him in every generation.
He has shown the strength of His arm,
He has scattered the proud in their conceit.
He has cast down the mighty from their thrones,
and has lifted up the lowly.

He has filled the hungry with good things,
and the rich He has sent away empty.
He has come to the help of His servant Israel
for He has remembered His promise of mercy,
the promise He made to our fathers,
to Abraham and his children forever.
Amen

Key Terms

Spiritual Betrothal
Spiritual Marriage

Chapter Sixteen

THE FRUITS OF UNION

Summary

The blessings that come in the unitive state aren't unique to those in a spiritual betrothal or spiritual marriage. They are present, albeit in a lesser form, for some time before. But once we enter into deep union with God, those blessings, or "fruits," take on a greater richness and power, a greater constancy.

These fruits come in many forms, affecting our relationship to work, to others, to God, and even to the devil. When we are in union with God, our apostolic activity is more effective and more powerful. A desire to please God, not others, moves us, which means we undertake all our actions with greater courage and greater freedom. The desire to do God's will comes readily, without hesitation, and a clear understanding of that will guides all our activity.

Reaching the state of union with God makes us more sensitive to others, and quickens our response to their needs. We also see more clearly, perceiving souls, truth, and even creation from God's vantage point. That seeing comes from continuous contact with God. His presence strengthens us, gives us a secure and lasting sense of peace, and protects us from the attacks of both man and the devil. His presence also illuminates our intellect and understanding, granting us supernatural knowledge, enhancing our natural knowledge, and bestowing upon us a profound understanding of both the things of God and the things of the world.

Above all, if we reach the state of union with God, we will receive a joy so immense and so powerful that it can take the form of ecstatic prayer and praise. This state of jubilation can become so intense at times that it has been likened to spiritual inebriation. It flows from close contact with God and testifies to the ongoing presence of the Holy Spirit both in the Church and our soul.

Questions for Comprehension

1. How, according to St. John of the Cross, does a soul in union with God respond to all "the things that happen to her," whether good or bad? Why does the soul respond that way?

2. How does the love experienced by a soul in union express itself?

3. What does St. Bernard advise a person to do who is confused about how much time to spend in contemplation and how much time to spend actively serving others?

4. If people want their work to become more fruitful, what does St. John of the Cross say they must do?

5. How, according to St. Catherine of Siena, is the love for God experienced by a soul in the unitive way different from the love experienced by souls in the purgative and illuminative ways?

6. How did St. Thérèse of Lisieux's love for creation lead her to greater love of God? How did entering the unitive stage deepen her love for creation?

7. What, according to St. Catherine, is the foundation for the peace and joy experienced by souls in the unitive way?

8. How does the devil respond to souls in union with God? What is the reason for that response?

9. Why might God, under certain circumstances, remove a sense of His presence from a soul in the state of spiritual marriage?

10. Describe three of the different ways that the extreme joy experienced by souls in union with God can manifest itself in this life?

Questions for Reflection

1. St. Bernard advised his brother monks to interrupt him, even if he was in contemplation, when someone had a genuine need. What does that advice tell us about the importance of serving others in the life of faith?

2. Look back at your answer to question number four above. How does St. John's advice differ from the opinion of the world? Judging by your actions, whose advice do you most often follow in that regard—St. John's or the world's?

3. Pope John Paul II, along with the saints and doctors, has said the joy of our salvation should be visibly and invisibly expressed in the life of the Church. Do you see evidence of that joy both in your life and the life of your parish? If so,

how? If not, why do you think that is? What can you do to change that?

More About—The Fruits of the Spirit

How can we know that the Holy Spirit is working within us, transforming us and preparing us for eternal joy? By the fruits His work bears in our lives.

Paragraph 1832 of the *Catechism of the Catholic Church* defines the fruits of the Holy Spirit as the "perfections that the Holy Spirit forms in us as the first fruits of eternal glory." Those perfections are both attitudes and actions, good habits and good inclinations that reflect the life of the Spirit within us.

And what are those fruits?

In Galatians 5:22–23, St. Paul lists nine of them:

- Charity
- Joy
- Peace
- Patience
- Kindness
- Generosity
- Gentleness
- Faithfulness
- And self-control

To that list, the Church has always added three more: goodness, modesty, and chastity.

Key Terms

Inebriation of the Holy Spirit

Chapter Seventeen

THERE'S ALWAYS MORE

Summary

In this life, no soul ever reaches the state of total and absolute perfection. Spiritual growth continues, even for those in the unitive way. Through both sufferings and blessings, God works in their souls, bringing them more and more into conformity with Christ and enabling them to participate more fully in both the sorrows of His crucifixion and the glories of His resurrection.

The sufferings of souls in the unitive way have a primarily redemptive purpose. In other words, these holy souls suffer more for the good of others than for their own good. Although their trials bear spiritual fruit for them as individuals, they bear more fruit for others. In their suffering, these souls become Christ's co-workers par excellence.

The sufferings themselves can take on many forms. They can come in the ways of illness or injury, relational difficulties, persecution, or rejection. They can also closely resemble the dark night that precedes spiritual betrothal—the dark night where a soul feels abandoned by God and bereft of any spiritual consolation. This was the type of trial St. Thérèse of Lisieux endured during the last year and a half of her life.

Regardless of which form they take, however, and no matter how severe or unjust they may seem, these trials ultimately express God's goodness and love. They are permitted for the good of that soul and the world. Because of that, the person who faces these final trials sees the suffering as a joy and blessing. They also know that when the time for endurance is done, they will receive a reward more joyous and beautiful than words can describe. It's that reward for which souls in the unitive state long—the beatific vision.

Nothing, other than death, can bring the satisfaction that seeing God face to face in heaven can bring—not the sacraments, not visions or locutions, not the joys of spiritual marriage. In heaven, no longer in need of purifying or perfecting, the saints understand and experience more deeply what it means to become "partakers of the divine nature" (2 Pet. 1:2–5), loving God as He loves them and receiving new and deeper insights into the mysteries of creation, salvation, and eternity. In death, their joy is complete. Their journey is complete. They have found the fulfillment of all desire.

Questions for Comprehension

1. What is the difference between the trials a soul endures before entering the unitive way and the trials endured by a soul who has already entered into a spiritual marriage with Jesus?

2. According to St. Catherine of Siena, what spiritual benefits can a person in the unitive way receive from the trials and sufferings that come from God?

3. As a person grows in holiness, how does the understanding of suffering change?

4. How did St. Thérèse respond to the profound darkness that engulfed her during the last year of her life? How did she understand that darkness?

5. What does it mean to "die of love"?

6. According to St. John of the Cross, how does a person's desire for death while in the unitive way differ from the desire for death souls in the purgative or illuminative way might experience?

7. Why does St. Bernard of Clairvaux say that no matter how much the Holy Spirit enlivens the sacraments, it is never enough for souls in the unitive way?

8. In your own words, describe the picture St. John and St. Bernard give of the beatific vision.

9. How, according to St. John of the Cross, does the Holy Spirit help prepare us for the beatific vision?

10. Is the idea of the beatific vision biblical? Write out two or three of the Scripture verses that support this teaching.

Questions for Reflection

1. As you've grown in faith, how has your understanding of suffering changed? Does the idea of "loving suffering" still strike you as strange? Why or why not? What do you think would help you more fully embrace suffering as a blessing?

2. What do St. Thérèse's love, humor, and joy in the face of great suffering teach you? What about Blessed Teresa of Calcutta's continued service through years of spiritual darkness—what

lesson can you learn from her? How do the experiences of those two women affect your understanding of holiness?

3. Does reading St. John and St. Bernard's descriptions of the beatific vision give you a greater desire for holiness? Why or why not? If your answer was "yes," what in your life are you willing to change so that you too can see God face to face? If your answer was "no," what do you think still needs to happen in your soul so that your answer can be "yes"? How can God make that change possible?

More About—Redemptive Suffering

When souls in the unitive state suffer, they suffer more for others than for themselves, obtaining grace and blessing for those in need of their intercession. But you don't have to be in a spiritual marriage with God in order to turn your suffering into a blessing for others. All you have to do is follow the advice of centuries of Catholic mothers and "offer it up."

When suffering comes your way, which it inevitably will if you choose to follow Christ ("If any man would come after me, let him deny himself and take up his cross and follow me" [Mt. 16:24])—you have two choices. You can rebel against the suffering—after reasonable efforts have been made to alleviate suffering that sometimes can and should be alleviated—or you can accept it. To accept it means to not question, to not demand understanding, to not rail at God and ask, "why me?" To accept it means to bow your head in submission to God and say, "Your will be done."

With His grace, this can be done. And with His grace, your acceptance of suffering will not only transform you, purging you of the vestiges of sin. It will also allow you to join your suffering to Christ's. United to Him, through God's gracious permission, your sufferings and sacrifices mysteriously "complete what is lacking in Christ's afflictions for the sake of his body, that is the Church" (Col. 1:24). They become more than a means of purgation. They become a means of blessing.

Key Terms

Dying of Love

A Final Encouragement

Read prayerfully again this very short chapter and be encouraged. You are called! Keep on to Journey's End!

GLOSSARY

Active Night of the Senses: The actions we take to detach ourselves from sinful habits and inordinate attachments to the things and pleasures of the world.

Active Night of the Spirit: The actions we take to detach ourselves from spiritual goods in order to move into deeper union with God.

Beatific Vision: The eternal and direct vision of God enjoyed by the blessed in heaven. In this vision, souls find total and complete happiness. It is the ultimate fulfillment of all that they longed for during their earthly life.

Contemplative Prayer: See "Mental Prayer."

Dark Night of the Senses: The purification of a soul by God from an inordinate attachment to the things and pleasures of the world or to a disordered attachment to others. This process of purification can lead a person to experience a sense of deprivation and emptying that is painful.

Dark Night of the Spirit: The deep purification of a soul from the roots of its sinful habits. In the dark night of the spirit, God acts in the soul directly, bringing about this purification both through earthly trials and through the temporary deprivation of spiritual consolations.

Despair: Thinking reform is hopeless and that one's sins or struggles are greater than God's mercy and grace. St. Bernard of Clairvaux called this the greatest of all evils.

Dying of Love: A type of death that can be experienced by a soul in the unitive state. This can occur when a soul reaches spiritual marriage then continues to grow closer to the Lord until it finally reaches the point where its love is so great that the soul actually leaves the body. The cause of this death is not illness or old age, but love.

Fear of the Lord: A respect and fear of a God who administers just punishment. It is based on a proper understanding of His holiness and our own ability to reject His love and mercy, violate His laws, and merit eternal separation from Him. The fear of the Lord is an experience that disposes souls to wisdom.

Filial Love: Literally, the love of a son or daughter. The love of God characteristic of the unitive stage.

Grace: The free and unmerited help that God gives us to enter into a relationship with Him and be conformed to His likeness. Through grace, we are able to turn from sin, develop the habit of virtue, carry out the work God has called us to, and participate in God's own life.

Illuminative Way: The general term used to describe the second stage of the spiritual life, a stage marked by continuing growth in faith.

Inebriation of the Holy Spirit: A state in which a soul is "intoxicated" with the joy of God's love. This joy can overflow in visible acts of rejoicing and jubilation.

Infused Contemplation: Recollection that is enhanced by an act of God. Through an act of grace, God gives the soul a deeper awareness of His presence and closeness, a loving knowledge of God.

Kiss of God: The giving of the Spirit that contains both light for the mind and fervor for the will.

Lectio Divina: Literally "sacred reading." The practice of combining the reading of Sacred Scripture with prayer. This method begins with reading Scripture until the mind and heart are elevated to the Lord, then either reflecting on what one has read or simply being in God's presence.

Meditation: Reflecting on a passage from Scripture, a scene from the Gospel, a mystery of the faith, or a passage from spiritual reading in order to increase one's love for the Lord.

Mental Prayer: Prayer said with the attention of the mind, where words may or may not be spoken. It consists of being aware of the presence of the Lord, understanding truths, or inflaming the will with acts of love. In this type of prayer, the eye of the soul is fixed on God. Also referred to as "Contemplative Prayer."

Moral Goods: The good of practicing the virtues, performing works of mercy, obeying the commandments, exercising good judgment, and having manners.

Mortal Sin: A violation of the moral law in a grave or serious matter carried out with both full knowledge and free consent. When committed, mortal sin destroys charity in a person's heart and cuts the person off from sanctifying grace.

Natural Goods: Goods that belong primarily to this world but have some transcendent qualities, i.e. beauty, grace, intelligence, and other talents.

Poverty of Spirit: A mental and emotional detachment from material things.

Prayer of Quiet: A type of prayer where the soul is absorbed in the Lord and the will is focused on Him, even though the intellect, memory, and imagination may still wander and be distracted.

Prayer of Union: A type of prayer where not only is the will united to the Lord but the other faculties of intellect, memory and imagination are absorbed in Him as well.

Purgative Way: The first general stage of the spiritual life marked by initial conversion, the rejection of sin, and the beginnings of piety and virtue.

Original Sin: The consequence of Adam's fall from grace inherited by all men and women. This consequence is the loss of original justice and holiness enjoyed by Adam and Eve before their fall, and an ongoing interior struggle within man—essentially a tendency towards sin– due to this lack of grace.

Recollection: The quieting of the soul and the focusing of the mind on God that must happen in order for a soul to enter into contemplative prayer.

Self-Knowledge: Knowledge of both the dignity of the human soul and its exalted destiny, as well as knowledge of the wounds and darkness sin has inflicted on it.

Sensory Goods: That which gives delight to the senses; i.e., what can be tasted, touched, smelled, seen, heard, and imagined.

Slavish Fear: A fear based not on love of God but on a dread of punishment, as well as a desire to avoid the pain of living in sin and to escape damnation.

Sleep of the Faculties: A level of prayer deeper than the prayer of quiet, with the will and the faculties focused on God, but not as deeply as in the prayer of union.

Spiritual Betrothal: The state that precedes spiritual marriage and in which signs are given that spiritual marriage will indeed occur. During this time, a person enjoys an abiding and attentive relationship with the Lord, marked by a sense of tranquility in the soul and frequent communication from God.

Spiritual Marriage: The highest state to which a soul can aspire in this life. A person who has reached this state enjoys a powerful and personal relationship with the Lord, where their entire being has been, in a sense, fused into His, just as His life has become an almost inextricable part of their own life.

Spiritual Goods: The infused gifts of God, both painful and delightful, which prepare us for union with God, i.e. "wounds of love," locutions, and visions.

Supernatural Goods: The gifts of the Holy Spirit given to build up the Body of Christ and benefit others, i.e. gifts of wisdom, healing, and prophecy.

Temporal Good: Goods that belong to this world, i.e. money, power, reputation, possessions.

Unitive Way: The third and final general stage of the spiritual life marked by a deep, habitual union with God.

Venial Sin: A violation of the moral law, but in a less serious matter than with mortal sin or without full knowledge and consent of what one is doing. Venial sin does not sever the relationship between God and a soul; charity can continue to subsist in a person who has committed a venial sin, although the sin both offends and wounds charity.

Vocal Prayer: Prayer said aloud. Usually understood to be the recitation of memorized prayers, such as the "Our Father" or "Hail, Mary."

Wounds of Love: Communications from God intended to increase a soul's desire for Him and which can be experienced as either painful or delightful.